GIRL TAKES DRASTIC STEP!

How Molly Lamb Bobak Became Canada's First Official Woman War Artist

Words by Jillian Dobson

Artwork by Genevieve Simms

NIMBUS
PUBLISHING
—— NIMBUS.CA ——

With admiration and gratitude in honour of Molly Lamb Bobak and the women of the CWAC, and with love for my mother, Lu Dobson.
—JILLIAN DOBSON

For my Mom, Audrey.
—GENEVIEVE SIMMS

Text copyright © 2024, Jillian Dobson
Artwork copyright © 2024, Genevieve Simms

Nimbus Publishing Limited
3660 Strawberry Hill Street, Halifax, NS, B3K 5A9
(902) 455-4286 nimbus.ca

Printed and bound in Canada

NB1650

Editor: Penelope Jackson
Art Direction: Heather Bryan & Whitney Moran
Design: Jenn Embree

Nimbus Publishing is based in Kjipuktuk, Mi'kma'ki, the traditional territory of the Mi'kmaq People.

Library and Archives Canada Cataloguing in Publication

Title: Girl takes drastic step! : how Molly Lamb Bobak became Canada's first official woman war artist / words by Jillian Dobson ; artwork by Genevieve Simms.
Names: Dobson, Jillian, author. | Simms, Genevieve, illustrator.
Identifiers: Canadiana (print) 20230588220 | Canadiana (ebook) 20230588239
    ISBN 9781774712788 (hardcover) ISBN 9781774712917 (EPUB)
Subjects: LCSH: Bobak, Molly Lamb, 1920-2014—Juvenile literature. | LCSH: Women painters—Canada—Biography—Juvenile literature. | LCSH: Painters—Canada—Biography—Juvenile literature. LCSH: War artists—Canada—Biography—Juvenile literature. | LCSH: World War, 1939-1945—Participation, Female—Juvenile literature. | LCGFT: Biographies. | LCGFT: Picture books.
Classification: LCC ND249.B554 D63 2024 | DDC j759.11—dc23

Nimbus Publishing acknowledges the financial support for its publishing activities from the Government of Canada, the Canada Council for the Arts, and from the Province of Nova Scotia. We are pleased to work in partnership with the Province of Nova Scotia to develop and promote our creative industries for the benefit of all Nova Scotians.

Molly always knew she was an artist.

When she was little, she loved to sketch and doodle
and draw. Her favourite subjects were Alice and Jersey.

At art school Molly learned about tints and textures. When she studied the paintings of famous artists, she didn't just *see* the brushstrokes of colour on the canvases—she *felt* them. They would wash over her like crashing waves, "blue strokes shattering around the edges, open, moving."

Paintings of the war by brave war artists gave Molly goosebumps.

When Molly saw a poster to recruit women into the army, she was transfixed. Courage tingled through her veins.

Was this her chance to become a war artist too?

Molly knew she had to try.
She joined the Canadian Women's Army Corps.

On her very first day in the army, she turned the flutters she felt about the enlistment process into sketches in her special diary, a headline journal.

On the second day, Molly asked to be assigned as an official war artist, but the commanding officers refused.

They didn't believe women belonged at the battlefront, and they said Molly had much to learn about the army.

Including how to sleep on a top bunk!

Molly was sent off to basic training with her platoon. After three days chugging across the country by train, she arrived in the frozen snow-globe landscape of Alberta.

Her teeth chattered as she covered her ears with numb hands. She trudged in her boots through ankle-deep snow.

Fierce wind burned her cheeks in the mornings. Hours of drill marching frosted her toes in the afternoons. But at night, warm in her blankets, she stayed up past lights out to sketch and doodle and draw what basic training was like.

Molly knew there had to be a way to convince her superiors she could be an official war artist, even if she was a woman.

She used her military wages to buy stamps and mailed envelopes stuffed with pictures to the CWAC Head Quarters in Ottawa. Proof she was good enough to be a war artist.

Their reply? She was reassigned...

...to the cafeteria. There she served countless cups of scalding coffee and sticky doughnuts. Then...

...to the kitchen. Where she peeled piles of potatoes and chopped bushels of turnips. Then...

...to the garage. She tried to block out the *clank-clank-clank* of the motors. She plugged out the smell of oil as she sketched grimy brakes and gears for repair manuals.

Molly was exhausted from the work. But by the streaks of moonlight peeking through her window, she sketched and doodled and drew more artwork to mail to newspapers, magazines, and art galleries.

After a weekend trip home, Molly lost her return ticket to the barracks. She searched high and low but missed her train.

Over a day late returning to her post, she was reported as "absent without leave," demoted, and reassigned...

...to the school of cookery, to illustrate recipes and meat-cutting charts for front line cooks.

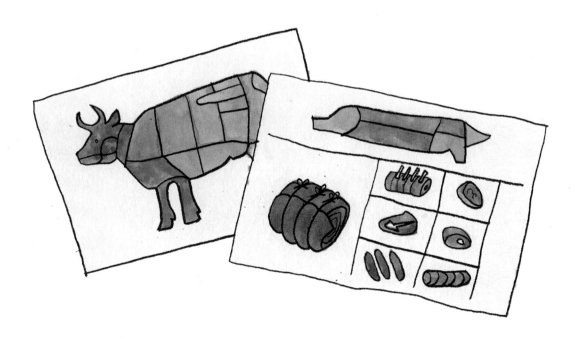

IF ONLY... MAY

As she sketched and doodled and drew, Molly's heart sank. Her shoulders slumped. Her dream to be an official war artist became hazy in the thick kitchen steam. Doubt swirled in her stomach. Should she give up trying?

"There just didn't seem much chance of it," she wrote in her journal. "It was a nice dream."

One day the butcher asked Molly to draw her portrait, and when a sergeant saw the drawing he invited Molly to report on the CWAC Track and Field Day. Her first real artist's assignment!

She ran the whole way there—right through a patch of poison ivy that sent her into scratching fits for days.

A new energy thrummed through her pencil. Curled on the corner of her bunk, Molly sketched and doodled and drew.

She painted two canvases that she carried by bus to Ottawa to enter in the National Gallery's Canadian Army Art Exhibition. The winner would be recommended as a war artist.

Molly was hopeful her dream was getting closer, but while she awaited the announcement, she was reassigned...

...to the Army Show department. At least she finally got to paint as part of her assignment. She didn't even mind it was bathroom scenery for a play to entertain the soldiers.

She also painted snakes and fish.

Molly beamed as she sketched and doodled and drew designs for hundreds of costumes. Working at the theatre filled her with hope, but she still longed to be an official war artist.

She mailed more envelopes stretched at the seams with drawings, and she asked each person she met whether there was a spot for her overseas.

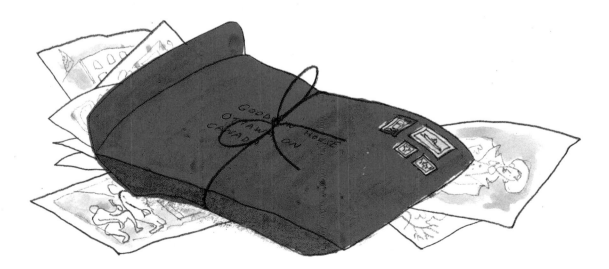

When Molly found out she was the runner-up in the art contest, she was so excited she saluted everyone and everything, including a traffic light! It took another year of waiting and training, but finally in May of 1945 Molly was reassigned...

...to travel east over the waves of the Atlantic Ocean to Europe and the front lines as Canada's first official woman war artist!

Molly travelled for months through the Netherlands, France, and Germany perched in the back of a squeaky old pickup truck.

She painted on a makeshift easel from the first tweet of the morning birds to the chirp of the evening crickets. She captured countless images of the CWAC women working for the war effort.

Molly achieved her dream of being an official war artist—
but really, she'd been an unofficial one since the day she
joined the army. In the sketches, doodles, and drawings
of her journal, she documented not just her own
headlines but also the experiences of many of the first
enlisted Canadian women in World War Two.

"There is endless material in one barracks alone,"
she wrote. "I never stopped drawing."

AUTHOR'S NOTE

Molly Lamb's positivity and determination to be a war artist in World War Two inspired me to write this story.

When I read about Molly's 226-page newspaper-style journal, which she regularly shared with her fellow CWACs, I was captivated by her sketches and drawings. The inside look at the first women enlisted into the Canadian war effort in 1942 fascinated me. Molly's journal explains her travels across the country, bouncing between postings, training, and cities, all the while highlighting the camaraderie with the other enlisted women and their efforts to learn their military roles. Molly brought to life details on everything from sharing a dormitory to the hours they spent doing drills and marching in formation to the wide variety of work CWAC women did to support the war effort. Before seeing Molly's work I'd never stopped to think about where the mail had been sorted, how many calls had been connected by operators, or who had typed the telegrams during the war. Molly provided an intimate look into the essential roles of women and brought their stories from behind the scenes to her headlines.

After the war Molly created over 100 works of war art and continued drawing daily until her death on March 2, 2014. Recognized as one of Canada's premier watercolour painters, she worked in many mediums, bringing a variety of subjects (including landscapes, wildflowers, and crowds) to life on canvas, in the pages of books, and in the minds of the next generation of artists through her teachings.

Do you know what your headlines will be?

SELECTED BIBLIOGRAPHY

Gewurtz, Michelle. *Molly Lamb Bobak: Life & Work*. Toronto: Art Canada Institute, 2019.

Gossage, Carolyn, ed. *Double Duty: Sketches and Diaries of Molly Lamb Bobak Canadian War Artist*. Toronto: Dundurn Press, 1992.

Greenfield, Nathan M. *Anything But A Still Life*. Fredericton: Goose Lane Editions, 2021.

Lamb, Molly. *W110278: The Personal War Records of Private Lamb, M., 1942-45*. Fonds at Library and Archives Canada.

Scoones, Anny. *Last Dance in Shediac: Memories of Mum, Molly Lamb Bobak*. Victoria: TouchWood Editions, 2013.

One of the real pages from Molly's headline journal, dated November 22, 1942.

The image on the left shows Lamb standing in the rain and on the right she's written information about her entry into the CWAC. The illustration below shows her working in the cafeteria.

The artwork is done in pencil and watercolour with pen and black ink on wove paper.

Previous page: Library Archives Canada 1993-168 NPC
Right: Library Archives Canada 1990-255 DAP 00003

ABOUT THE AUTHOR & ILLUSTRATOR

PHOTO BY DOROTHY PUDDESTER

JILLIAN DOBSON delights in discovering stories in the everyday. She's gathered tales through various unofficial and official roles. Jillian has lived in Alberta and Quebec and now lives in Richmond Hill, Ontario, with her incredible husband, their two inspiring children, and a cuddly cat. She's thankful for her supportive family and writing partners, Heather Camlot and Loretta Garbutt.

PHOTO BY JENNIFER GRIFFITHS

GENEVIEVE SIMMS has been illustrating for a variety of clients in editorial, advertising, and book publishing since 2006. She also has a background in architecture. Originally from St. John's, Newfoundland, Genevieve currently lives in Edmonton, Alberta, with her partner, Josh, and their dog, Birdy.